Success With

Addition & Subtraction

SCHOLASTIC

Editor: Ourania Papacharalambous
Cover design by Tannaz Fassihi; cover illustration by Kevin Zimmer
Interior design by Cynthia Ng
Interior illustrations by Doug Jones (4, 27, 31, 35, 43, 44); Stephen Brown (5, 14, 18, 21, 25, 29, 30);
Cynthia Ng (6, 7, 11, 13, 16, 17, 19, 20, 28, 45)
All other images © Shutterstock.com

ISBN 978-1-338-79827-2
Scholastic Inc., 557 Broadway, New York, NY 10012
Copyright © 2022 Scholastic Inc.
All rights reserved. Printed in the U.S.A.
First printing, January 2022
2 3 4 5 6 7 8 9 10   150   29 28 27 26 25 24 23

INTRODUCTION

Parents and teachers alike will find *Scholastic Success With Addition & Subtraction* to be a valuable educational tool. These practice pages incorporate engaging puzzles, games, and picture problems that will both stimulate and encourage children as they improve their math skills. On page 4, you will find a list of the key skills covered in the activities throughout this book. Children are challenged to sharpen their addition and subtraction skills, complete graphs, solve problems, and more. Remember to praise children for their efforts and successes!

TABLE OF CONTENTS

Grade-Appropriate Skills Covered in *Scholastic Success With Addition & Subtraction: Grade 1*

Use addition and subtraction within 20 to solve word problems involving situations of adding to, taking from, putting together, taking apart, and comparing, with unknowns in all positions.

Apply properties of operations as strategies to add and subtract.

Understand subtraction as an unknown-addend problem.

Relate counting to addition and subtraction.

Add and subtract within 20, demonstrating fluency for addition and subtraction within 10.

Determine the unknown whole number in an addition or subtraction equation relating three whole numbers.

Understand that the two digits of a two-digit number represent amounts of tens and ones.

Add within 100, including adding a two-digit number and a one-digit number.

Organize, represent, and interpret data with up to three categories; ask and answer questions about the total number of data points, how many in each category, and how many more or less are in one category than in another.

Funny Dog

Add. Color the picture using the Color Key.

Color Key

1	white
2	orange
3	black
4	tan
5	purple
6	green
7	blue
8	brown
9	yellow
10	red

Lovey Ladybugs

Write a number sentence to show how many spots each ladybug has.

___1___ + ___2___ = ___3___

____ + ____ = ____

____ + ____ = ____

____ + ____ = ____

____ + ____ = ____

____ + ____ = ____

____ + ____ = ____

____ + ____ = ____

____ + ____ = ____

 Color the ladybug that has the greatest number of spots red.
Color the ladybug that has the least number of spots blue.

Beautiful Bouquets

Look at the number on each bow. Draw more flowers to match the number written on the bow. Then, color the bows that have an even number yellow. Color the bows that have an odd number purple.

An **even number** can be divided evenly into two whole numbers. An **odd number** cannot be divided evenly into two whole numbers.

Juggling Act

Read each problem. Cross out the number of balls. Then, write how many are left.

3 – 1 = 2

7 – 4 = ____

4 – 2 = ____

5 – 3 = ____

9 – 6 = ____

6 – 5 = ____

Trucking Along

Subtract. Color the picture using the Color Key.

Color Key

0	white
1	brown
2	**black**
3	green
4	**purple**
5	**orange**
6	yellow
7	**blue**
8	**red**

Night Lights

Subtract. Connect the dots from greatest to least.

$10 - 3 = \boxed{}$ •

$9 - 1 = \boxed{}$ $8 - 2 = \boxed{}$

$10 - 1 = \boxed{}$ •   • $9 - 4 = \boxed{}$

$10 - 0 = \boxed{}$ •   • $7 - 3 = \boxed{}$

$5 - 3 = \boxed{}$

$6 - 5 = \boxed{}$ •   • $8 - 5 = \boxed{}$

Subtract. Connect the dots from greatest to least.

$10 - 0 = \boxed{}$ •   • $9 - 8 = \boxed{}$

$7 - 5 = \boxed{}$

$10 - 1 = \boxed{}$ •

$10 - 7 = \boxed{}$

$10 - 2 = \boxed{}$ •

$7 - 0 = \boxed{}$ • $6 - 2 = \boxed{}$

$9 - 3 = \boxed{}$ •   • $9 - 4 = \boxed{}$

Hop to It

Add or subtract. Trace the number line with your finger to check your work.

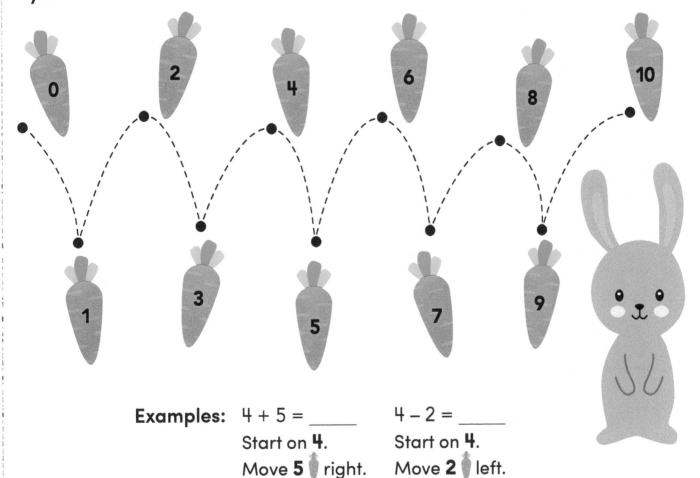

Examples:

$4 + 5 = \underline{\hspace{1cm}}$
Start on **4**.
Move **5** 🥕 right.

$4 - 2 = \underline{\hspace{1cm}}$
Start on **4**.
Move **2** 🥕 left.

$7 - 3 = \underline{\hspace{1cm}}$	$9 - 6 = \underline{\hspace{1cm}}$	$2 + 0 = \underline{\hspace{1cm}}$
$5 + 5 = \underline{\hspace{1cm}}$	$8 - 7 = \underline{\hspace{1cm}}$	$4 + 3 = \underline{\hspace{1cm}}$
$10 - 4 = \underline{\hspace{1cm}}$	$6 + 2 = \underline{\hspace{1cm}}$	$7 - 2 = \underline{\hspace{1cm}}$

Kickboard Matchup

Add or subtract. Draw a line to match kickboards with the same answer.

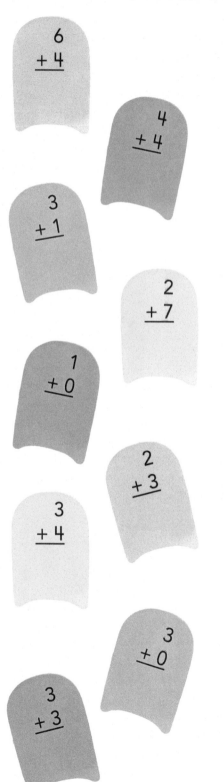
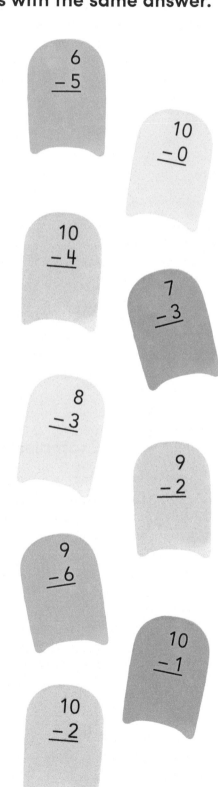

Blast Off

Add or subtract. Then use the code to answer the riddle below.

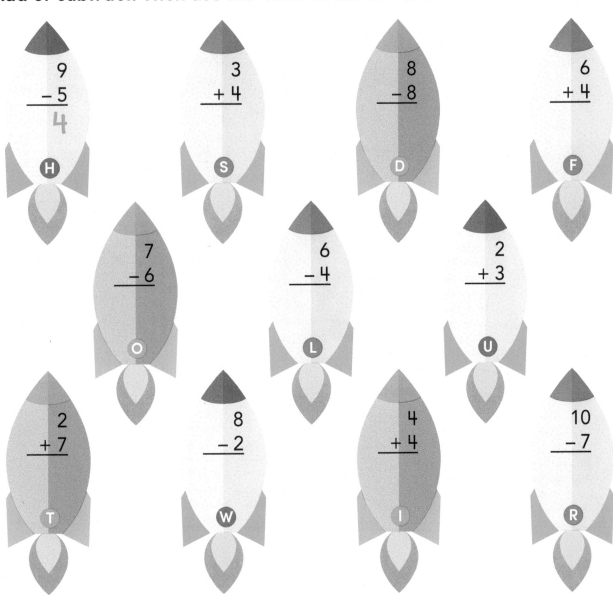

```
  9        3        8        6
- 5      + 4      - 8      + 4
---      ---      ---      ---
  4
  H        S        D        F
```

```
  7        6        2
- 6      - 4      + 3
---      ---      ---
  O        L        U
```

```
  2        8        4       10
+ 7      - 2      + 4      - 7
---      ---      ---      ---
  T        W        I        R
```

How is an astronaut's job unlike any other job?

,

| __ | __ | __ | | __ | __ | __ | | __ | __ |
| 8 | 9 | 7 | | 1 | 5 | 9 | | 1 | 10 |

| __ | __ | __ | __ | | __ | __ | __ | __ | __ | __ |
| 9 | 4 | 8 | 7 | | 6 | 1 | 3 | 2 | 0 | ! |

(H under the 4)

Shapes on a Snake

Write the number for each shape. Add or subtract.

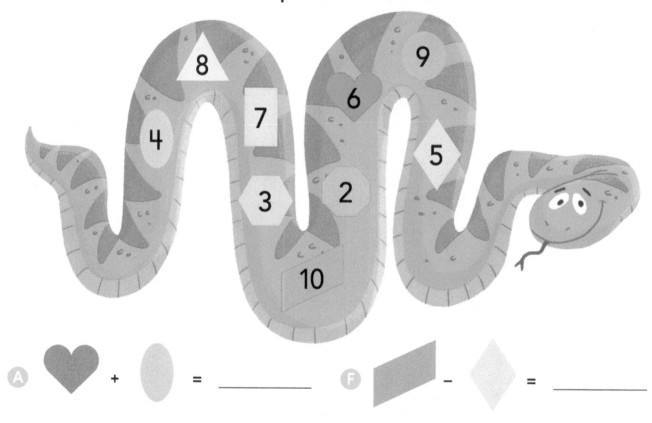

A ♥ + ⬭ = _____   F ▱ − ◇ = _____

B ⬭ − ⯃ = _____   G ⬭ + ♥ = _____

C ▭ + ⯃ = _____   H ⯃ + ⬡ = _____

D ◇ + ⬡ = _____   I ♥ − ⬭ = _____

E △ − ▭ = _____   J ▱ − ⬡ = _____

Out on the Town

Color a box on the graph for each item in the picture. Then, answer the questions below. Circle the plus or minus sign to add or subtract.

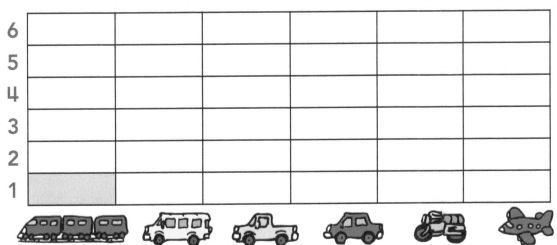

1 How many 🚗 and ✈️ altogether? $6 \oplus 2 = 8$

2 How many 🏍️ and 🚆 in all? ___ $\overset{+}{-}$ ___ = ___

3 How many more 🚗 than 🚌 ? ___ $\overset{+}{-}$ ___ = ___

Planes... Trains...

**Answer the questions.
Circle the plus or minus sign
to add or subtract.**

B

There are **7** boxes on the truck. Then, **4** boxes fall on the street. How many boxes are left on the truck?

___ +/− ___ = ___ boxes

A

There are **7** cars in the parking lot. Then, **3** more cars park there, too. How many cars are there in all in the lot?

_7_ ⊕/− _3_ = _10_ cars

C

There are **10** planes waiting on the runway. Then, **6** planes take off. How many planes are left on the runway?

___ +/− ___ = ___ planes

D

There are **8** girls and **2** boys on the bus. How many more girls than boys are on the bus?

___ +/− ___ = ___ more girls

E

There are **5** people in the first car and **4** people in the second car. How many people in all?

___ +/− ___ = ___ people

Slice It Up

Add. Color the picture using the Color Key.

Color Key

14	brown
15	green
16	red
17	yellow
18	tan

Leap on Over

Add. To show the frog's path across the pond, color each lily pad green if the sum is greater than 10.

10 + 1 =

6 + 4 =

6 + 9 =

5 + 2 =

9 + 2 =

7 + 0 =

5 + 5 =

10 + 4 =

3 + 7 =

7 + 6 =

4 + 3 =

5 + 4 =

3 + 8 =

2 + 2 =

8 + 8 =

Flying High

Add down and across to find the missing number.

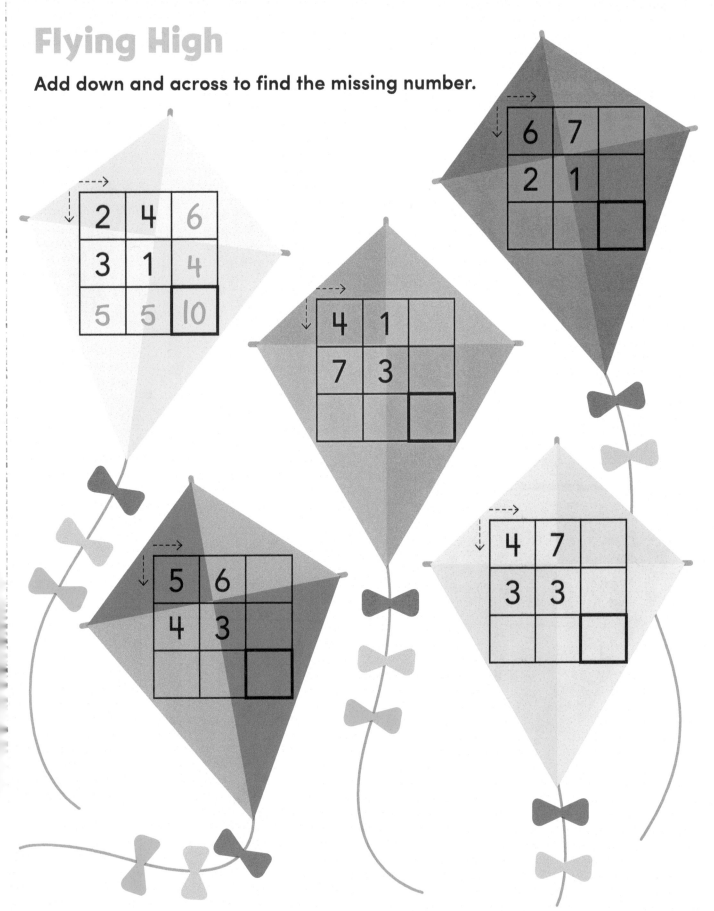

Double Dips

Write the doubles that equal the number on the cone.

8
8
16

8

12

16

18

2

4

6

10

14

☆ Circle the answer. When adding doubles, the sum will always be: **even   odd**

Not Far From Home

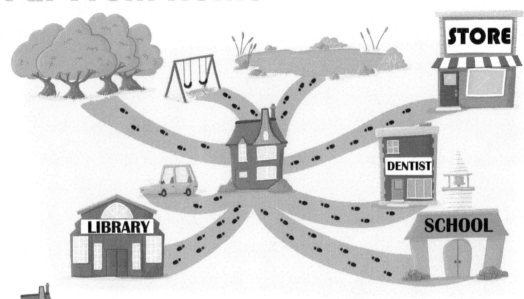

Start at  . **Write the numbers of steps. Add.**

steps to + steps home = _____ steps   steps to + steps home = _____ steps

STORE 🏠 7 + 7 = 14	SCHOOL 🏠 _____ + _____ = _____
🌳 🏠 _____ + _____ = _____	(swing) 🏠 _____ + _____ = _____
LIBRARY 🏠 _____ + _____ = _____	(car) 🏠 _____ + _____ = _____
DENTIST 🏠 _____ + _____ = _____	(pond) 🏠 _____ + _____ = _____

Scholastic Success With Addition & Subtraction • Grade 1

Break the Code

Subtract.

6	13	17	18	15
− 2	− 7	− 7	− 9	− 8

11	9	14	11	7
− 9	− 4	− 6	− 8	− 6

- -

Use the answers above to solve each problem.

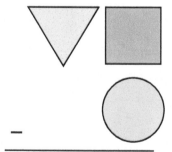   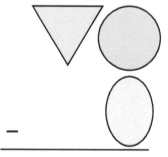   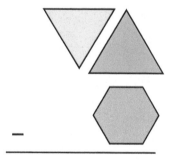

The Big Search

Subtract. Circle the difference.

11 – 7 = five three (four)	14 – 9 = nine one five
13 – 6 = six nine seven	16 – 5 = twelve thirteen eleven
18 – 9 = eleven ten nine	17 – 11 = seven six ten
15 – 5 = ten seven five	12 – 9 = three two four
12 – 4 = six eight nine	11 – 9 = three five two

Find each circled number in the word puzzle. Look → and ↓.

```
(f  o  u  r)  h  i  o  n  e  g  s  k  m
 i  f  o  n  t  g  y  f  a  f  u  e  z
 f  t  l  u  e  j  s  i  x  s  b  x  t
 t  t  w  e  l  v  e  v  k  s  t  l  h
 e  p  n  i  n  e  w  e  j  e  r  t  i
 e  d  n  g  q  i  h  r  y  v  a  q  r
 n  v  h  h  o  t  h  r  e  e  c  s  t
 d  m  k  t  c  w  b  t  e  n  t  r  e
 x  d  i  p  g  o  a  c  p  f  i  s  e
 c  e  l  e  v  e  n  a  b  z  o  v  n
 b  w  u  d  i  f  f  e  r  e  n  c  e
```

See if you can find these number words: **twelve, fifteen, thirteen, subtraction, difference.**

Race Through the Facts

Add or subtract.
The race car that ends with the highest number wins the race!

$7 + 2 =$ _____ $- 4 =$ _____ $- 3 =$ _____ $+ 9 =$ _____

$12 - 3 =$ _____ $- 6 =$ _____ $+ 2 =$ _____ $+ 9 =$ _____ $+ 5 =$ _____ $- 8 =$ _____

$+ 4 =$ _____ $- 5 =$ _____ $+ 7 =$ _____ $- 6 =$ _____ $+ 3 =$ _____ $- 2 =$ _____ $+ 7 =$ _____

$+ 6 =$ _____ $- 9 =$ _____ $+ 1 =$ _____ $+ 4 =$ _____ $- 8 =$ _____ $+ 1 =$ _____ $- 11 =$ _____

$+ 2 =$ _____ $+ 3 =$ _____ $- 3 =$ _____ $- 5 =$ _____ $+ 13 =$ _____ $- 7 =$ _____ $+ 3 =$ _____

Little Snacks

Help the elephant find the peanuts. Add or subtract. Then, follow the maze through the even answers.

13 − 6 =

16 − 9 =

4 + 5 =

START
2 + 2 =

14 − 8 =

10 − 7 =

3 + 7 =

9 + 4 =

13 − 5 =

15 − 6 =

16 − 6 =

11 + 3 =

17 − 8 =

7 + 5 =

18 − 6 =

8 + 3 =

5 + 2 =

9 + 9 =

A Nutty Bunch

Add or subtract. Circle the nut if the answer matches the squirrel.

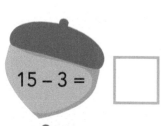 $15 - 3 =$ □

 $6 + 7 =$ □

 13

 $11 + 2 =$ □

 $17 - 4 =$ □

 $13 + 4 =$ □

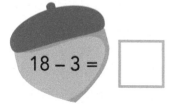 $18 - 3 =$ □

 17

 $9 + 6 =$ □

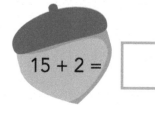 $15 + 2 =$ □

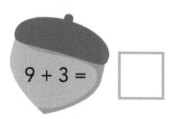 $9 + 3 =$ □

 $8 + 3 =$ □

 11

 $15 - 4 =$ □

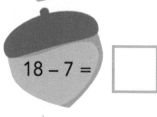 $18 - 7 =$ □

Penguin Parade

Add or subtract.

Row 1:
- 5 + 7
- 8 + 3
- 15 − 5
- 18 − 9
- 11 − 3
- 12 − 5

Row 2:
- 9 − 7
- 12 − 8
- 5 + 1
- 16 − 8
- 13 − 3
- 7 + 5

Row 3:
- 12 − 9
- 11 − 5
- 13 − 4
- 7 + 6
- 18 − 3
- 11 + 7

Row 4:
- 15 − 2
- 4 + 7
- 12 − 3
- 12 − 5
- 8 − 3
- 12 − 9

Flying Families

Fill in the missing number for each family. Use the numbers from the box.

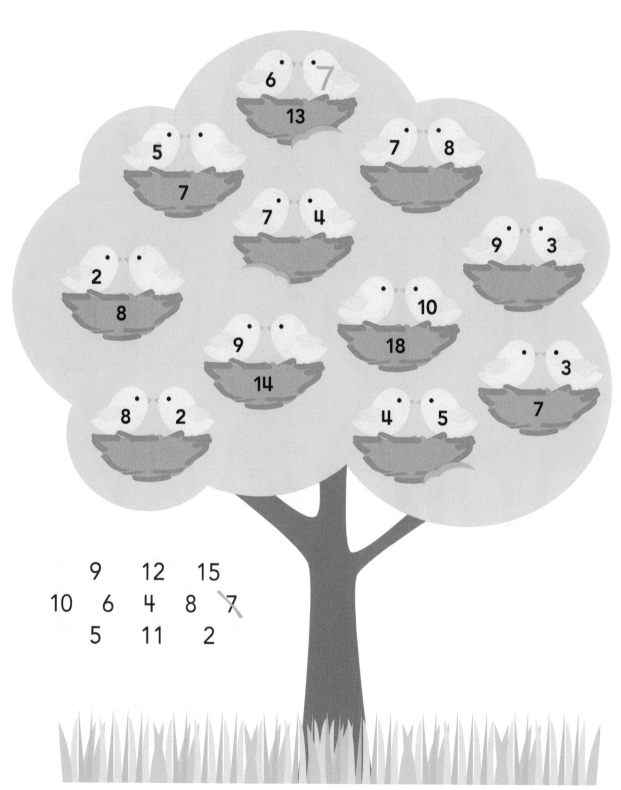

© Scholastic Inc.

Colorful Flowers

Color a box on the graph for each item in the picture.

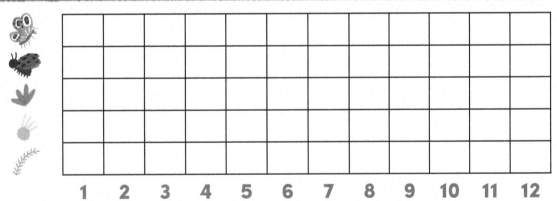

1. Which flower is found the most?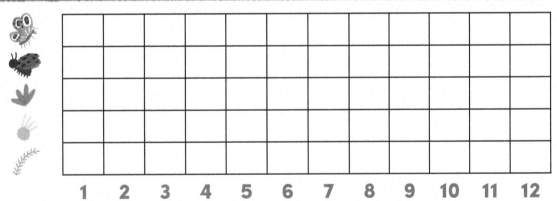

2. How many and altogether? _____ + _____ = _____

3. How many more than ? _____ – _____ = _____

4. How many insects in all? _____ + _____ = _____

5. How many more than ? _____ – _____ = _____

6. How many and altogether? _____ + _____ = _____

What a Treat!

Find the number in the mouse and cheese. ☐

Find the sum of the numbers in the cheese.

_____ + _____ + _____ = _____

Find the sum of the numbers in the mouse.

_____ + _____ + _____ = _____

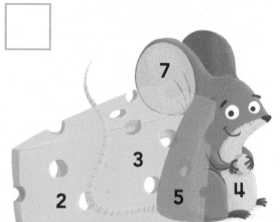

Find the number in the rabbit and carrot. ☐

Find the sum of the largest number in the rabbit and the smallest number in the carrot.

_____ + _____ = _____

Find the difference between the largest and smallest number in the carrot.

_____ − _____ = _____

 Find the sum of all the numbers in the cheese and carrot.

_____ + _____ + _____ + _____ + _____ + _____ = _____

By the Seashore

Use the code below to write each missing number. Add.

93
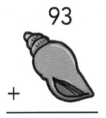
+ _____

82
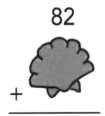
+ _____

14
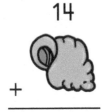
+ _____

21
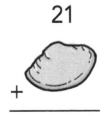
+ _____

53
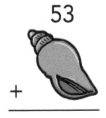
+ _____

45
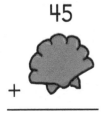
+ _____

73

+ _____

36
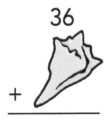
+ _____

61
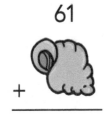
+ _____

32
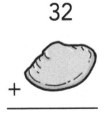
+ _____

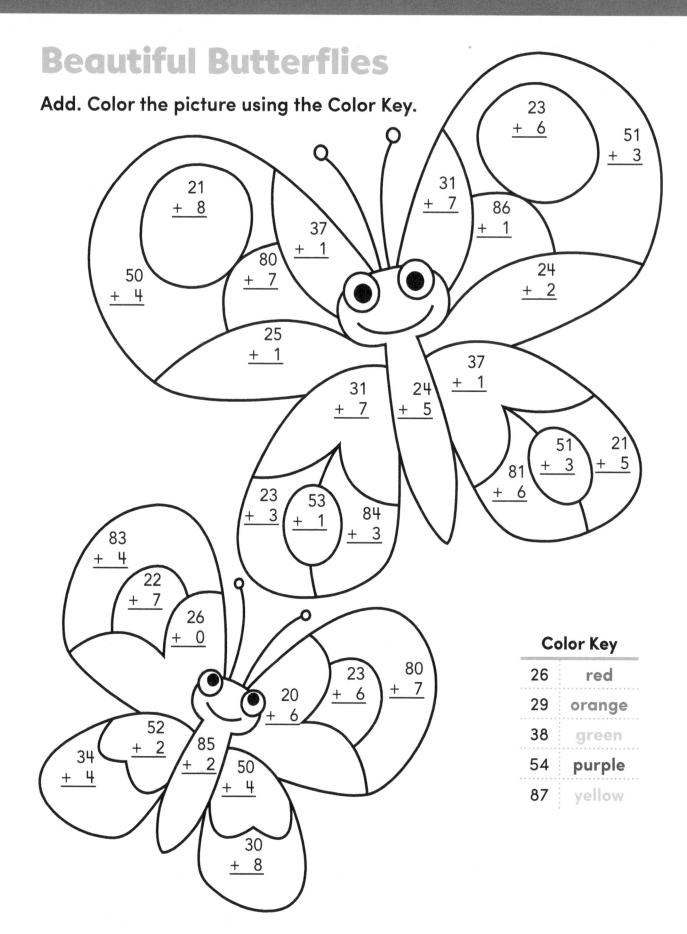

Beautiful Butterflies

Add. Color the picture using the Color Key.

Color Key

26	red
29	orange
38	green
54	purple
87	yellow

© Scholastic Inc.

Sail Away

Find each addition sentence. Add.

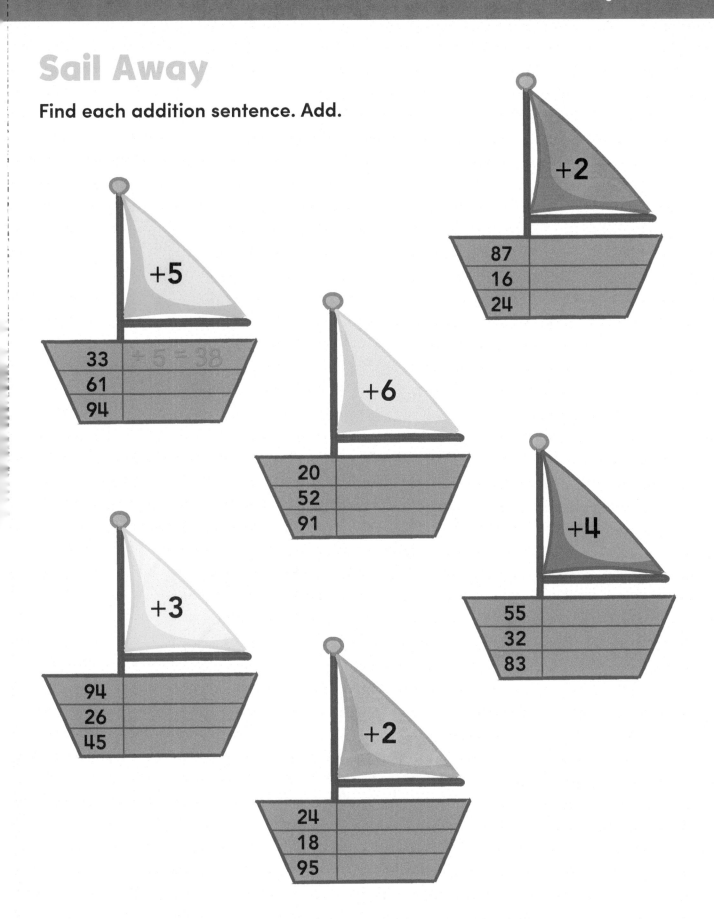

+2

87	
16	
24	

+5

33	+ 5 = 38
61	
94	

+6

20	
52	
91	

+4

55	
32	
83	

+3

94	
26	
45	

+2

24	
18	
95	

Dino-Math

Subtract. Color the picture using the Color Key.

Color Key

16	red
22	orange
34	purple
57	blue
73	yellow
85	green

Butterfly Friends

Subtract. Remember: The larger number always goes on top!

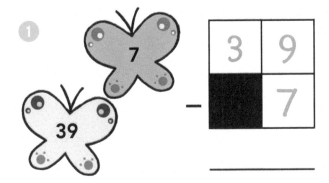

1.
$$\begin{array}{c} 3\ 9 \\ -\ \ \ 7 \\ \hline \end{array}$$

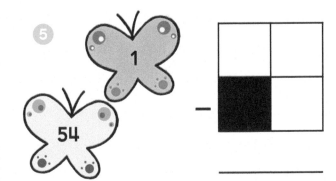

5.

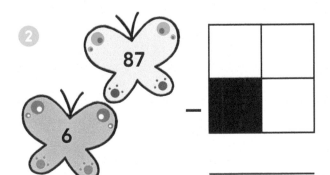

2.

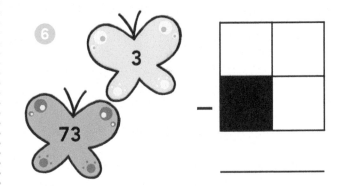

6.

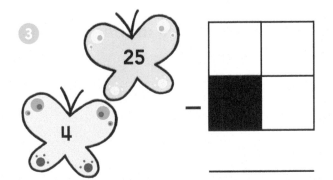

3.

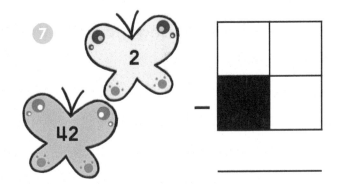

7.

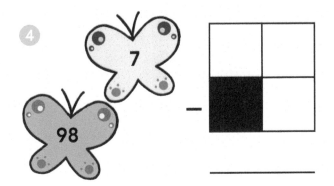

4.

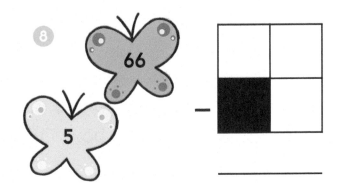

8.

Treasure Island

Subtract.

43 − 1	95 − 5	79 − 3	36 − 4	89 − 7	66 − 3	83 − 2
59 − 9	37 − 2	24 − 3	27 − 6	42 − 1	90 − 0	55 − 2
33 − 3	84 − 4	28 − 8	71 − 1	62 − 2	68 − 3	77 − 3

Use the clues to find the gold, the ship, and the treasure in the boxes above.

Find the gold. The difference is greater than **50** and less than **55**. Color the box with the gold yellow.

Find the ship. The difference is greater than **30** and less than **35**. Color the box with the ship orange.

Find the sunken treasure. The difference is greater than **70** and less than **75**. Color the box with the treasure red.

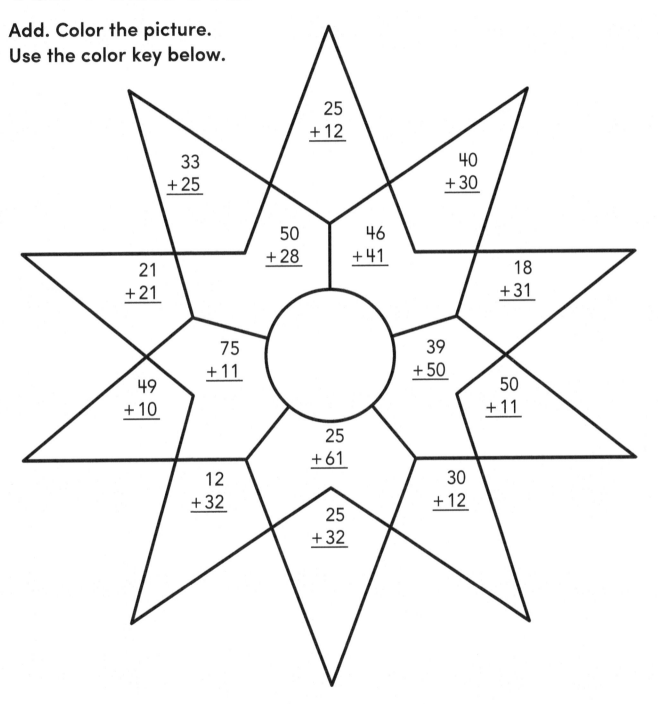

Ten-Point Star

Add. Color the picture.
Use the color key below.

If the sum is between	Color the space
1 and 50	orange
51 and 70	yellow
71 and 100	red

Fill in the other spaces with colors of your choice.

Designer Diamond

Add. Color the picture.
Use the color key below.

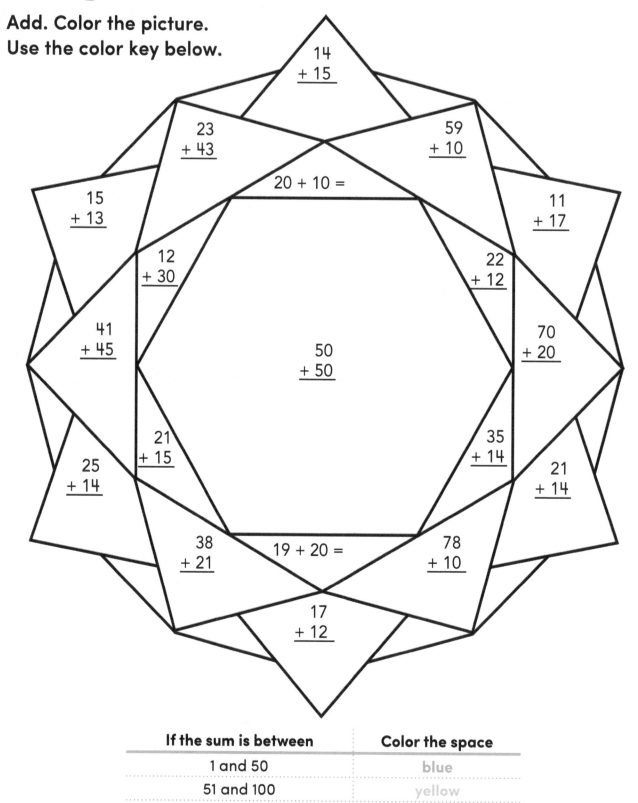

If the sum is between	Color the space
1 and 50	blue
51 and 100	yellow

Fill in the other spaces with colors of your choice.

Riding on Air

Add. Color the picture using the Color Key.

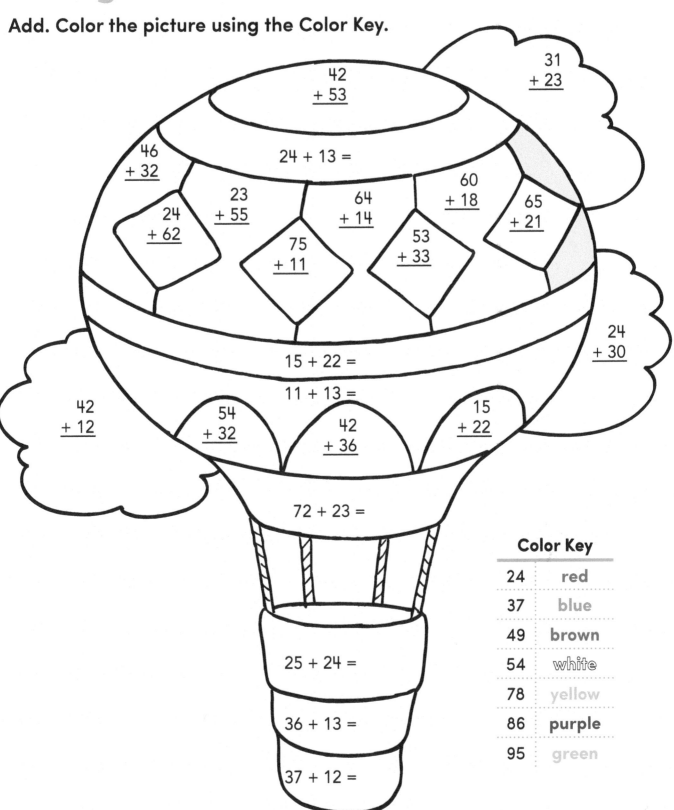

Color Key

24	red
37	blue
49	brown
54	white
78	yellow
86	purple
95	green

Amazing Maze

Subtract. Color the picture. Use the color key below.

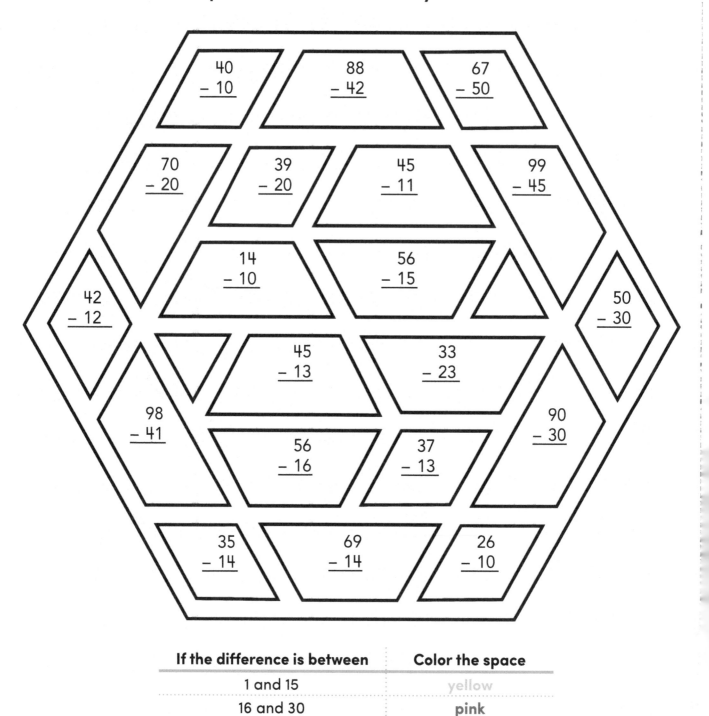

If the difference is between	Color the space
1 and 15	yellow
16 and 30	pink
31 and 45	purple
46 and 60	blue

Fill in the other spaces with colors of your choice.

Have a Ball

Subtract.

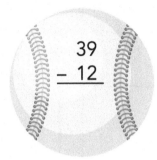
$$\begin{array}{r} 39 \\ -\ 12 \\ \hline \end{array}$$

$$\begin{array}{r} 97 \\ -\ 23 \\ \hline \end{array}$$

$$\begin{array}{r} 59 \\ -\ 18 \\ \hline \end{array}$$

$$\begin{array}{r} 77 \\ -\ 12 \\ \hline \end{array}$$

$$\begin{array}{r} 79 \\ -\ 52 \\ \hline \end{array}$$

$$\begin{array}{r} 81 \\ -\ 11 \\ \hline \end{array}$$

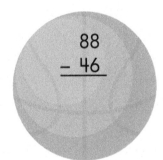
$$\begin{array}{r} 88 \\ -\ 46 \\ \hline \end{array}$$

$$\begin{array}{r} 63 \\ -\ 10 \\ \hline \end{array}$$

$$\begin{array}{r} 58 \\ -\ 43 \\ \hline \end{array}$$

$$\begin{array}{r} 46 \\ -\ 23 \\ \hline \end{array}$$

$$\begin{array}{r} 35 \\ -\ 24 \\ \hline \end{array}$$

$$\begin{array}{r} 68 \\ -\ 35 \\ \hline \end{array}$$

$$\begin{array}{r} 32 \\ -\ 12 \\ \hline \end{array}$$

$$\begin{array}{r} 74 \\ -\ 54 \\ \hline \end{array}$$

$$\begin{array}{r} 69 \\ -\ 54 \\ \hline \end{array}$$

$$\begin{array}{r} 83 \\ -\ 52 \\ \hline \end{array}$$

Color the Bow

Do the subtraction problems in the picture below.
Then use the Color Key to color each answer.

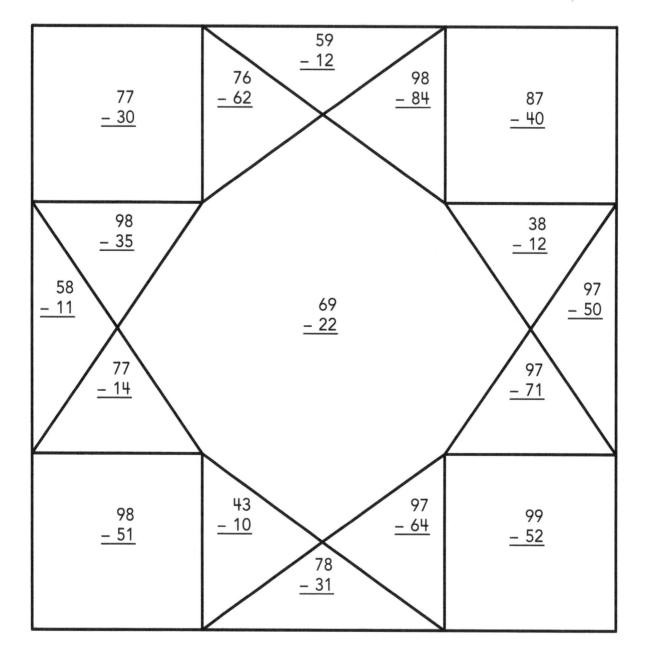

Opposites Attract

Add or subtract. Draw a line to connect the magnets with the same answer. Read the words in each connecting set of magnets.

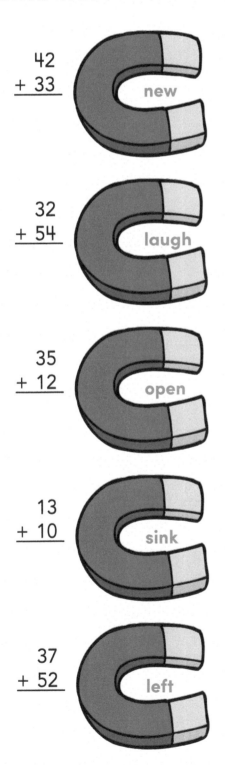

42
+ 33

new

32
+ 54

laugh

35
+ 12

open

13
+ 10

sink

37
+ 52

left

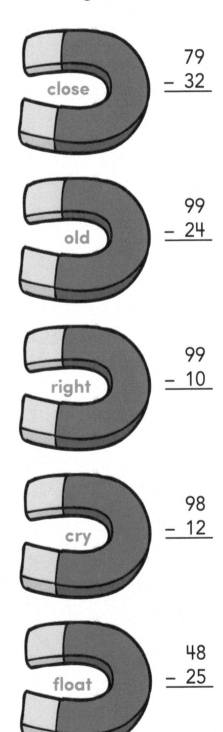

79
– 32

close

99
– 24

old

99
– 10

right

98
– 12

cry

48
– 25

float

Let the Sun Shine

Add or subtract. Then use the code to fill in the letters
to finish each sun fact.

13	26	34	42	57	63	71	76	85	88
f	a	s	g	r	e	l	h	t	i

$$\begin{array}{cccc} 13 & 32 & 57 & 89 \\ +21 & +53 & -31 & -32 \end{array}$$

The sun is a ____ ____ ____ ____ .

$$\begin{array}{ccccc} 30 & 98 & 12 & 97 & 99 \\ +41 & -10 & +30 & -21 & -14 \end{array}$$

The sun gives ____ ____ ____ ____ ____ and

$$\begin{array}{cccc} 34 & 51 & 88 & 42 \\ +42 & +12 & -62 & +43 \end{array}$$

____ ____ ____ ____ to Earth.

$$\begin{array}{cccc} 88 & 56 & 49 & 30 \\ -17 & +32 & -36 & +33 \end{array}$$

Without the sun, there would be no ____ ____ ____ ____ .

Fishbowl Families

Add or subtract. Circle the fish that does not belong with the family.
Hint: Look at the tens place.

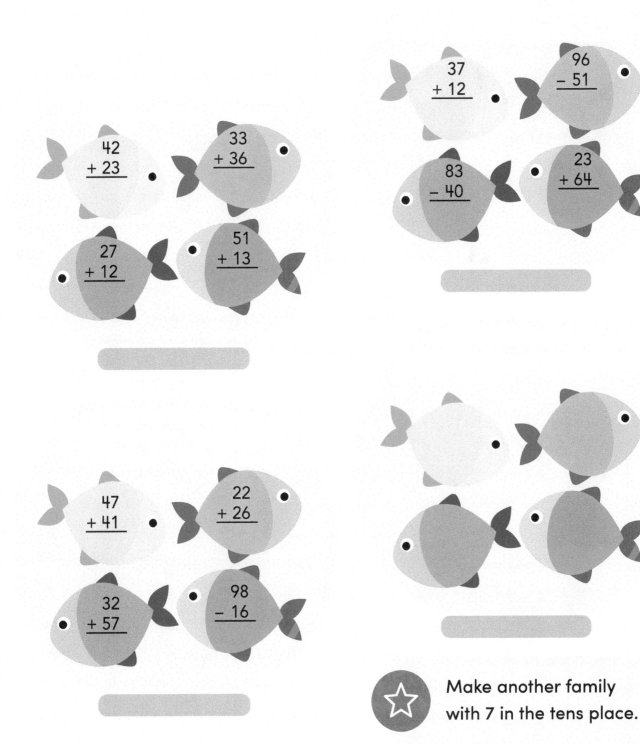

$$37 + 12$$

$$96 - 51$$

$$83 - 40$$

$$23 + 64$$

$$42 + 23$$

$$33 + 36$$

$$27 + 12$$

$$51 + 13$$

$$47 + 41$$

$$22 + 26$$

$$32 + 57$$

$$98 - 16$$

⭐ Make another family with 7 in the tens place.

ANSWER KEY

Page 5

Page 6
$1 + 2 = 3$, $2 + 3 = 5$, $7 + 3 = 10$;
$3 + 4 = 7$, $1 + 0 = 1$, $3 + 2 = 5$;
$1 + 1 = 2$, $4 + 4 = 8$; $1 + 3 = 4$;
Extra Activity: The ladybug with 10 spots should be colored red. The ladybug with 1 spot should be colored blue.

Page 7
Check that the correct number of flowers have been drawn.
7: needs 3 **10:** needs 5 **4:** needs 1
6: needs 2 **9:** needs 5 **5:** needs 3
8: needs 4 **3:** needs 2
The bows with 4, 6, 8, and 10 should be yellow. The bows with 3, 5, 7, and 9 should be purple.

Page 8
2, 3, 2; 2, 3, 1

Page 9

Page 10

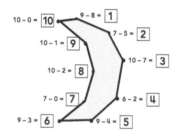

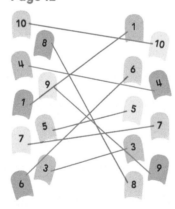

Page 11
4, 3, 2; 10, 1, 7; 6, 8, 5

Page 12

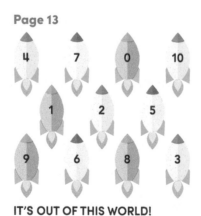

Page 13

IT'S OUT OF THIS WORLD!

Page 14
A. $6 + 4 = 10$ **F.** $10 - 5 = 5$
B. $9 - 2 = 7$ **G.** $4 + 6 = 10$
C. $7 + 2 = 9$ **H.** $2 + 3 = 5$
D. $5 + 3 = 8$ **I.** $6 - 4 = 2$
E. $8 - 7 = 1$ **J.** $10 - 3 = 7$

Page 15

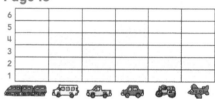

1. $6 + 2 = 8$ **2.** $3 + 1 = 4$
3. $6 - 4 = 2$

Page 16
A. $7 + 3 = 10$ **B.** $7 - 4 = 3$
C. $10 - 6 = 4$ **D.** $8 - 2 = 6$
E. $5 + 4 = 9$

Page 17

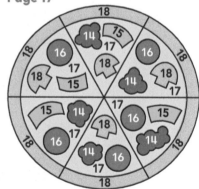

Page 18

Page 19

2	4	6
3	1	4
5	5	10

4	1	5
7	3	10
11	4	15

6	7	13
2	1	3
8	8	16

5	6	11
4	3	7
9	9	18

4	7	11
3	3	6
7	10	17

Page 20
8, 8; 4, 4; 6, 6; 8, 8; 9, 9; 1, 1; 2, 2;
3, 3; 5, 5; 7, 7; **Extra Activity:** even

Page 21
7 + 7 = 14, 5 + 5 = 10, 8 + 8 = 16,
6 + 6 = 12; 9 + 9 = 18, 3 + 3 = 6,
2 + 2 = 4; 4 + 4 = 8

Page 22
4, 6, 10, 9, 7; 2, 5, 8, 3, 1;
5 − 2 = 3, 9 − 3 = 6, 7 − 5 = 2, 8 − 1 = 7;
12 − 6 = 6, 16 − 8 = 8, 14 − 5 = 9

Page 23
four, five; seven, eleven; nine, six;
ten, three; eight, two

Page 24
7 + 2 = 9 − 4 = 5 − 3 = 2 + 9 = 11 + 5 = 16
− 8 = 8 + 4 = 12 + 6 = 18 − 9 = 9 + 1 = 10
+ 4 = 14 − 8 = 6 + 2 = 8 + 3 = 11 − 3 = 8;
12 − 3 = 9 − 6 = 3 + 2 = 5 + 9 = 14 − 6 =
8 + 7 = 15 − 6 = 9 + 3 = 12 − 2 = 10 + 7 =
17 + 1 = 18 − 11 = 7 − 5 = 2 + 13 = 15 − 7
= 8 + 3 = 11

Page 25

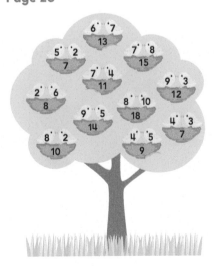

Page 26
Check that child has circled
the correct nuts.
15 − 3 = 12, 6 + 7 = 13,
11 + 2 = 13, 17 − 4 = 13;
13 + 4 = 17, 18 − 3 = 15,
9 + 6 = 15, 15 + 2 = 17;
9 + 3 = 12, 8 + 3 = 11,
15 − 4 = 11, 18 − 7 = 11

Page 27
5 + 7 = 12, 8 + 3 = 11, 15 − 5 = 10,
18 − 9 = 9, 11 − 3 = 8, 12 − 5 = 7;
9 − 7 = 2, 12 − 8 = 4, 5 + 1 = 6,
16 − 8 = 8, 13 − 3 = 10, 7 + 5 = 12;
12 − 9 = 3, 11 − 5 = 6, 13 − 4 = 9,
7 + 6 = 13, 18 − 3 = 15, 11 + 7 = 18;
15 − 2 = 13, 4 + 7 = 11, 12 − 3 = 9,
12 − 5 = 7, 8 − 3 = 5, 12 − 9 = 3

Page 28

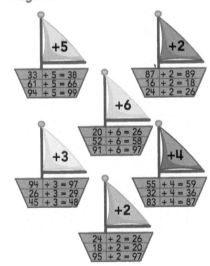

Page 29

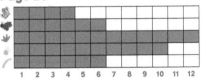

1. First flower should be circled.
2. 6 + 10 = 16   **3.** 12 − 4 = 8
4. 4 + 6 = 10   **5.** 12 − 6 = 6
6. 4 + 10 = 14

Page 30
5; 3 + 2 + 5 = 10; 4 + 5 + 7 = 16;
6; 7 + 2 = 9; 6 − 2 = 4
Extra Activity: 5 + 3 + 2 + 6 + 2 + 3 = 21

Page 31
93 + 6 = 99, 82 + 4 = 86, 14 + 5 = 19,
21 + 7 = 28, 53 + 6 = 59; 45 + 4 = 49,
73 + 3 = 76, 36 + 3 = 39, 61 + 5 = 66,
32 + 7 = 39

Page 32

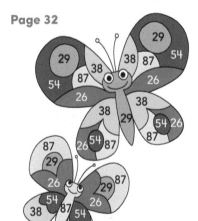

Page 33

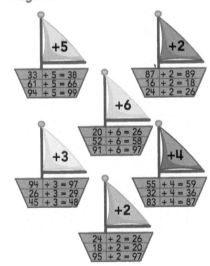
33 + 5 = 38
61 + 5 = 66
94 + 5 = 99

87 + 2 = 89
16 + 2 = 18
24 + 2 = 26

20 + 6 = 26
52 + 6 = 58
91 + 6 = 97

94 + 3 = 97
26 + 3 = 29
45 + 3 = 48

55 + 4 = 59
32 + 4 = 36
83 + 4 = 87

24 + 2 = 26
18 + 2 = 20
95 + 2 = 97

Page 34

Page 35

1. 39 – 7 = 32   **2.** 87 – 6 = 81
3. 25 – 4 = 21   **4.** 98 – 7 = 91
5. 54 – 1 = 53   **6.** 73 – 3 = 70
7. 42 – 2 = 40   **8.** 66 – 5 = 61

Page 36

42, 90, 76, 32, 82, 63, 81;
50, 35, 21, 21, 41, 90, 53;
30, 80, 20, 70, 60, 65, 74;
The box with 53 should be colored yellow. The box with 32 should be colored orange. The box with 74 should be colored red.

Page 37

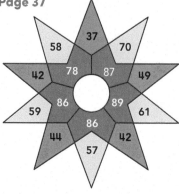

Page 38

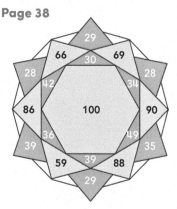

Page 39

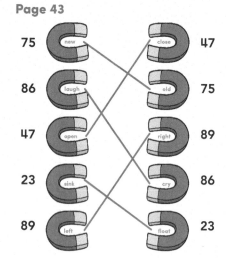

Page 40

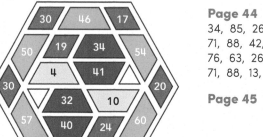

Page 41

39 – 12 = 27, 97 – 23 = 74,
59 – 18 = 41, 77 – 12 = 65;
79 – 52 = 27, 81 – 11 = 70,
88 – 46 = 42, 63 – 10 = 53;
58 – 43 = 15, 46 – 23 = 23,
35 – 24 = 11, 68 – 35 = 33;
32 – 12 = 20, 74 – 54 = 20,
69 – 54 = 15, 83 – 52 = 31

Page 42

(quilt square with numbers: 47, 14, 47, 14, 47; 63, 26; 47, 47, 47; 63, 26; 47, 33, 47, 33, 47; 47)

Page 43

75 new   close 47
86 laugh   old   75
47 open   right 89
23 sink   cry   86
89 left   float 23

Page 44

34, 85, 26, 57; star;
71, 88, 42, 76, 85; light;
76, 63, 26, 85; heat;
71, 88, 13, 63; life

Page 45

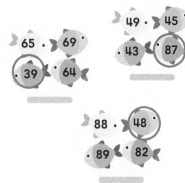

Extra Activity: Answers will vary.